DEFEATING YOUR ADVERSARY IN THE COURT OF HEAVEN

DEFEATING YOUR ADVERSARY IN THE COURT OF HEAVEN

PRAYING MEDIC

INKITY PRESS™

Inkity Press, 137 East Elliot Road, #2292, Gilbert, AZ 85234

This book and other Inkity Press titles can be found at:
InkityPress.com and **PrayingMedic.com**

Available from Amazon.com, CreateSpace.com, and other retail outlets.

For more information visit our website at **www.inkitypress.com** or email us at **admin@inkitypress.com** or **admin@prayingmedic.com**

ISBN-13: 978-0998091211 (Inkity Press)
ISBN-10: 0998091219

Printed in the U.S.A.

Acknowledgments

I WOULD LIKE TO THANK the many people who helped in the development of this book by providing feedback during my public discussions and by leaving comments on the articles I've posted. You know who you are. I greatly value your experiences, your insights and your encouragement.

I'd like to thank my talented wife for her editorial help with the manuscript and for her design of the book interior and cover.

I'm grateful to my editor and friend Lydia Blain for her editorial help.

TABLE OF CONTENTS

1   What Are the Courts of Heaven? 9

2   What is the Court of Accusation? 15

3   Why Should I Appear in the Court of Accusation? 17

4   How Do I Appear in the Court of Accusation? 23

5   Hearing the Accusation 25

6   Responding to the Accusation 29

7   Asking for a Verdict 33

8   Enforcing the Verdict 35

9   Court of Accusation Protocol 39

10 Testimonies 41

11 Closing Thoughts 49

CHAPTER ONE

WHAT ARE THE COURTS
OF HEAVEN?

IN THE LAST FEW YEARS, there has been growing interest among believers in learning how to operate in the Courts of Heaven. For those who are unfamiliar with the Courts of Heaven, I'll provide a brief explanation of what they are and why we may want to visit them.

The Courts of Heaven are places where the legal proceedings of heaven are carried out. Cases are brought before a Judge, witnesses testify, and rulings are handed down. The legal systems of society that we're familiar with did not arise randomly, nor were they invented by man. The concepts of justice, law, courts, and legal proceedings existed in heaven first, and over the millennia our society learned of them and copied them. Our modern system of legal justice was modeled after the Courts of Heaven.

Defeating Your Adversary in the Court of Heaven

We see glimpses of the Courts of Heaven and their proceedings both in the Old and New Testaments. The seventh chapter of the book of Daniel gives us a view of God as a Judge who sits upon a fiery throne, presiding over a heavenly Court. In Psalm 82, the Lord says He judges among the hosts of heaven. In the scriptures, Jesus is portrayed not just as our savior, but as our legal advocate or attorney:

> *And if anyone sins, we have an Advocate with the Father, Jesus Christ the righteous. (1 Jn 2:1)*

Satan is portrayed as our accuser or the one who prosecutes us:

> *Then he showed me Joshua the high priest standing before the angel of the Lord, and Satan standing at his right side to accuse him. (Zech 3:1 NIV)*

It's clear from these passages that Satan and his company of evil spirits have access to a Court of Heaven where they can accuse us, and through those accusations, torment us. Would we not expect God to allow us access to the same Court?

Many people I know have had breakthrough in the area of physical healing after appearing in the Court of Heaven when prayer alone didn't seem to help. Just as many people have reported sudden, positive outcomes in legal matters after their appearance in court. There are definite benefits, but if we are going to receive the outcome we want, we need to appear in the right court.

In the same way that there are different courts on earth, each with their own jurisdiction, there are different courts in heaven, each designed to hear certain types of cases. The Court of Scribes is a court where the records of heaven are kept. The Court of Angels is where you can be assigned angels to assist you in fulfilling your divine mandates. As children of God we've been given authority to appear in His courts. As we mature, we may be invited to appear in any of the higher courts, but we are not invited to appear in all of them at first.

Most people begin exercising their judicial authority by appearing in what is referred to as the Court of Accusation or the Mobile Court. Any believer may appear in this court. It's suitable for hearing the most common cases we're likely to be involved in. If you're sick, if you've suffered a legal setback, if your business is hampered by governmental red tape, or if in some other way God's plan for your life is being opposed by an adversarial spirit, this is where your case will be heard. One reason why we appear in this court first, is to learn how the courts function. Although the power of a verdict rendered in this court is as powerful as any court, the proceedings here are informal and extensive knowledge isn't required.

The Scope of This Book

The focus of this book is limited to presenting your case in the Court of Accusation (or the Mobile Court). We will discuss only one type of case and that is when an accusation is brought against you by an evil spirit. We will not cover matters such as regional or national intercession, or warfare against territorial spirits. Those issues are not appropriate for the Court of Accusation. They're handled in other Courts using different protocols. I may write other books that teach how to exercise our judicial authority in those Courts.

Warning

Engaging the Courts of Heaven provides certain opportunities for believers and with those opportunities, certain temptations, which must be handled with wisdom.

Some of us will wrongly identify another person as our adversary. We'll become convinced that they must be prosecuted in the Courts of Heaven. The motive may be revenge or merely a desire for justice, but such actions will only cause us more trouble. The Bible is clear that our warfare is not against flesh and blood (other humans) but against spiritual forces of darkness in heavenly places (see Eph 6:12).

A person whose soul is so wounded that they would seek divine judgment upon their fellow man instead of mercy is not in need of justice, but emotional healing. If you're wise, you will never consider opposing another human in the Courts of Heaven. I'd like to share a testimony that illustrates what can happen if you do.

In one of my public discussions, a man said he took his ex-wife to the Court of Heaven. The Judge asked if he was certain he wanted to proceed. He said he was. He said the venue suddenly changed and he appeared in a different court with a different judge, named Anubis. (Anubis is an Egyptian God believed to have power over the afterlife.) The outcome of his case was not what he wanted. This is why I believe a warning is necessary.

The Court of Accusation should only be used to hear cases that pertain to harassment, oppression, and affliction by evil spirits, and nothing else.

CHAPTER TWO

WHAT IS THE COURT OF ACCUSATION?

THE HEAVENS CONTAIN MANY PLACES where we may appear to observe or participate in the governmental and legal proceedings of God's kingdom. The Court of Accusation is the Court used by our adversary when he brings an accusation against us. Those who call it the Mobile Court have given it this name because of its availability. Unlike the higher Courts which are convened at particular times for particular people to hear particular types of cases, the Mobile Court can be convened anywhere at any time for just about any type of case. In that sense, it is the most flexible and the most mobile of all the Courts of Heaven.

When a believer appears in the Mobile Court to face an accuser, their activities tend to be somewhat informal. Although it is often with fear and anxiety that we appear in a human court, there is little reason to be fearful in the Court of Accusation. The judge and Jesus are on your side and they want to see you vindicated. There are a few guidelines to keep in mind when you appear in this Court, but they do not concern your *behavior* as much as the particular way in which you *respond* to an accusation. As long as you follow a few simple principles there is little that can go wrong when you appear in this Court.

CHAPTER THREE

WHY SHOULD I APPEAR IN THE COURT OF ACCUSATION?

BELIEVERS WHO APPEAR IN THE Court of Accusation do so for different reasons. Some appear there to have an illness removed. Some go there to have their finances restored. Some have appeared there to have obstructions to legal proceedings removed. Some appear there to have business dealings and contracts approved. One reason to go there is to get help with delivering an afflicted person from a demon.

When dealing with an evil spirit, they should respond to a believer operating under the authority of Jesus. When a demon does not respond, it should cause you to suspect that there is a legal problem which needs to be resolved. Going to the Court of Accusation may reveal the reason why a demon has refused to leave.

Defeating Your Adversary in the Court of Heaven

Although the reason why we may want to appear in Court could be just about anything, it is generally the accusation of an evil spirit that summons us there. Before we discuss how our adversary accuses us I'd like to address a legal matter that merits our attention.

In our earthly system, when someone believes you've violated a law, they can file a report with the police and the appropriate court will hear the accusation against you. Your responsibility is to appear in court to answer the accusation. You may bring witnesses and you may dispute the accusation or you can admit guilt, but you must appear in court. If you don't appear in court, the judge will issue a warrant for your arrest. The warrant allows the police to come to your home or work and arrest you. Once they have you in custody they will bring you before the judge to answer the accusation. If your case is heard and you refuse to appear, or if you do appear, but refuse to respond to the accusation, you will be found guilty. Even if you are not guilty of the charges, a default verdict of guilt will be rendered if you fail to respond appropriately. The only way for you to be exonerated is to appear in court and respond to the accusation.

If you understand this process, it will help you understand how the Courts of Heaven operate. The point we must keep in mind is that if someone is accused and they fail to appear and answer the accusation, they cannot be exonerated, even if they are not guilty.

In most of the cases we'll encounter, an evil spirit will appear in the Court of Accusation and accuse us of some wrongdoing. When the accusation goes unanswered, the accuser wins by default and uses this victory to afflict or oppress us. We're going to look at two cases from the Bible that illustrate how this process works. The first example is found in the book of Job.

In the first chapter of the book of Job, we read where Satan accused Job of serving God for selfish reasons. It isn't known whether this accusation was true, because Job didn't appear there to answer the charge. God defended Job's honor and reminded Satan that he was a righteous man, but that's all He was able to do. He wasn't able to exonerate Job because he had not appeared there to face his adversary and answer the accusation.

God then made the observation that all which Job had was in Satan's hands. Some have interpreted this as God giving Satan permission to afflict Job, but I don't think that's what happened. God merely pointed out the obvious fact that because Job didn't appear to answer the accusation, he could not be cleared of the charges. Job's failure to appear gave Satan the victory, which he then used to attack Job. The next chapter of the book shows a similar event. Satan once again accused Job of wrongdoing. God once again defended Job's honor, but because he didn't appear to answer the accusation, Job could not be exonerated. Satan again won by default and used the victory to attack Job.

The sickness, loss of family, and loss of property Job suffered stands as a poignant reminder of what the enemy can do to us if we fail to respond to his accusations. Now let's look at a similar case that had a different outcome.

In the third chapter of the book of Zechariah, Satan appeared and brought an accusation against Joshua the high priest. This time the accused made an appearance to answer the accusation and Zechariah appeared with him to witnesses the proceeding.

Here is how the case played out:

> *Then the angel showed me Joshua the high priest standing before the angel of the Lord. The Accuser, Satan, was there at the angel's right hand, making accusations against Joshua. And the Lord said to Satan, "I, the Lord, reject your accusations, Satan. Yes, the Lord, who has chosen Jerusalem, rebukes you. This man is like a burning stick that has been snatched from the fire."*
>
> *Joshua's clothing was filthy as he stood there before the angel. So the angel said to the others standing there, "Take off his filthy clothes." And turning to Joshua he said, "See, I have taken away your sins, and now I am giving you these fine new clothes."*
>
> *Then I said, "They should also place a clean turban on his head." So they put a clean priestly turban on his head and dressed him in new clothes while the angel of the Lord stood by. (Zech 3:1-5 NLT)*

Immediately after he made the accusation against Joshua, the Lord rebuked Satan and rejected the accusations. Joshua was dressed in dirty clothing, which symbolized his sin and was likely the reason why Satan had accused him. The Lord had his dirty clothing (sin) removed and had him dressed in fine clothing. Even though Joshua was likely guilty of the accusation, once he appeared in heaven and faced his accuser, the Lord was able to take away his guilt.

In the fourth chapter of the book of Ephesians, the apostle Paul reminded believers not to let the sun go down on their anger because it gave the enemy a foothold (Eph 4:26-27). He informed them that holding onto emotions like anger provided an opportunity for the enemy to accuse them before God. The accuser could then use the unanswered accusation as a way to afflict or oppress them.

This problem must be dealt with in two ways:

First, we must realize that Satan is a legalist. He and his evil spirits are continually looking for any fault in us that they can use to accuse us before God. We must live in a way that gives our enemy nothing to accuse us of. Second, when the enemy does accuse us, we must go to the Court of Accusation and answer the charge.

The Court of Accusation is convened to hear an accusation that is being brought against us by an evil spirit. The Court provides an opportunity for us to respond to and be exonerated of the accusation. This is the only type of activity we should engage in while we are in this Court.

CHAPTER FOUR

HOW DO I APPEAR IN THE
COURT OF ACCUSATION?

ALTHOUGH IT MAY SEEM LIKE we would need to have great
prophetic insight or well-developed spiritual gifts, appearing in the
Court of Accusation is easier than you might imagine. You have
a spirit that exists in the spiritual world. Your spirit can engage
the spiritual realms at any time. This includes the realms of
heaven. If you've been born again by the Spirit of God, you
have full access to them right now. God the Father dwells in the
heavenly realms. Jesus said that He is the door to the Father. We
can access the realms of heaven, the Father, and the Courts any
time we want, through Jesus.

Activities in the spiritual world, the realms of heaven, and the
Courts are generally sensed by our spirit through images we see
in our mind and thought impressions or words and phrases that

we hear with our spiritual ears. Some of this activity is picked up by our other spiritual senses.

Sometimes we'll sense an accusation being brought against us in the Mobile Court by feeling as though we're being accused. It's easy to write off these feelings as just random, meaningless feelings, but it is likely that our spirit has sensed an accusation and the feelings are prompting us to appear there to answer it.

Most of us have received prayer for a particular situation involving our health, our finances, or some other matter and it seemed as if there was an obstacle preventing us from receiving God's promise. It's possible there was a legal issue that the enemy was using to obstruct the process. Whenever you sense that God's will is being obstructed, you may go to the Mobile Court and ask if there is an accusation being brought against you.

Appearing in the Mobile Court to answer an accusation is a simple process. The first step is to address the Judge and ask for the Court to be convened. You can think this in your mind or you can say it out loud. The next step is to ask for your accuser to appear. When your accuser appears you may sense his presence in any number of ways. Some people see an image in their mind of a creature. I often see something like a dark cloud beside me. The accuser can appear in almost any way imaginable, but he will appear in a way that will let you know he has arrived in Court. A friend shared a testimony saying that when she first went to the Mobile Court there was more than one accuser and they were being guarded by a large angel. The number of accusers and how they appear will be different for each person.

CHAPTER FIVE

HEARING THE ACCUSATION

ONCE YOUR ACCUSER HAS APPEARED, you may ask to hear the accusation against you. I've often seen the accusation appear before I asked for it to be stated. Friends have reported that as soon as they arrived in court, the Judge asked how they wanted to plead, even before they heard the accusation. Be prepared for anything when you first arrive in Court, but take heart in knowing that your defense will nearly always follow the same script.

Accept the fact even before you arrive in court that the accusation you're going to hear will be true, even if you don't recall committing the sins mentioned or feel like the accusation is true. Your defense does not require you to dispute the accusation and you may have a negative outcome if you attempt to.

There are many ways in which you might perceive an accusation once it's been revealed. How it is perceived is unique to each person and it can be different each time you appear in Court. The accusation may come as just a single word or several words that you "hear" such as blasphemer, adulterer, murder, liar, etc. Some people hear the words as thoughts in their mind. Others may see them in their mind's eye as literal words. Sometimes I see the accusations as words that appear to swirl around in the cloud that represents my accuser.

I have on occasion asked for my "book" to be opened (see Dan 7:10). There are books that are kept in heaven which record the events of our lives. A person's book (or scroll) may contain many things, including the destiny God has planned for them. The one that appears in the Court of Accusation usually contains the sins that they've committed, displaying a written record of the accusation. It will sometimes be seen lying on a table. I've heard people say that the Judge had their book when they appeared in court. You may need to ask for it to be brought forth if you don't see it. Once you see it, you can ask for it to be opened. If you're able to read any of the text, it will probably reveal the accusation. (This is only if you decide you want to have the accusation revealed through your book. It is not mandatory. It's just one of many ways the accusation can be revealed.)

Sometimes the accusation brought against you is a general accusation about sins you've committed. Other times it may pertain to the situation you are currently engaged in. It may point out an ungodly attitude, a selfish motive, or some weakness you habitually struggle with. Try not to be discouraged by what is revealed in the accusation. It's easy to feel unworthy or even feel as if the accuser has a perfect right to harass you. When I go to the Court I tend to pay little attention to the accusation. Most times, it doesn't have any bearing on my plans. I already know what I'm going to do, so the reading of the accusation is, in some respects, just a formality. Once you've heard the accusation the next step is responding to it.

CHAPTER SIX

RESPONDING TO THE ACCUSATION

AN IMPORTANT PRINCIPLE TO KEEP in mind is that the Court of Accusation has a different way of achieving justice than courts on earth. When you appear in an earthly court, you're there to be exonerated. That's often done by disputing accusations that are brought against you. In the Court of Accusation, the goal is to be exonerated, but it's not done by disputing an accusation.

Every one of us has sinned. We are guilty and without excuse. But Jesus died for our sins. The blood that was shed when He was crucified paid the price to remove our guilt. Our vindication in the Courts comes when we accept that the blood of Jesus is the only thing that can take away our guilt and make us righteous before the Judge. Jesus is our attorney. His blood is our defense.

In general, there is one strategy you'll want to employ when responding to an accusation. Jesus gave us part of that strategy in the Sermon on the Mount:

"Agree with your adversary quickly, while you are on the way with him, lest your adversary deliver you to the judge, the judge hand you over to the officer, and you be thrown into prison." (Matt 5:25)

Notice in this passage that Jesus referred specifically to officers of the Courts. Although it's in our nature to defend ourselves, the Court of Accusation is one place where we must resist this temptation. When responding to an adversary, never dispute an accusation. To do so may lead to serious consequences and as believers, it's not necessary for us to argue. Simply agree with the accusation and move on to the next part of the process.

After you've agreed with the accusation, the next step is to remove its effect. This is done by acknowledging that the blood of Jesus is your defense. You can do this in a number of ways, but you're simply stating the fact that you come before the Court not in your own righteousness, but in the righteousness provided by the blood of Jesus. You're allowing His blood to impute its righteousness to you. This removes your guilt, takes away the effect it had on you, and silences your accuser. There are a few situations that may require other types of responses, which I'll outline next.

If an accusation only pertains to you, then you can respond to it through the blood of Jesus. If the accusation involves repetitive patterns of ungodly behavior that are likely to bring further accusations and force you to return to Court, it's a good idea to repent of the behavior.

Sometimes an accusation involves something we said years ago. When an action causes a person to suffer severe shame, embarrassment, or emotional trauma, they may make an inner vow of some sort to protect themselves. An example is abuse by a leader. Some people have suffered abuse at the hands of church leadership and have vowed never again to trust Christian leaders. These vows, which are often made in ignorance, become a legal contract and can be used by an adversary. When we stand in Court we may hear our own words being used against us. If the accusation involves something you've said, simply renounce your agreement with those words, repent of the mindset and behavior connected to it, and let the blood of Jesus be your defense.

You may go to Court and find that the accusation involves the illegal, immoral, or ungodly behavior of your parents, grandparents, or other descendants. Satanism, witchcraft, Freemasonry, human trafficking, and involvement in slavery are common examples. If the accusation involves someone other than yourself, you may need to repent on their behalf. Additionally, because their behavior has negatively affected you, it may be helpful to forgive them and release them of any responsibility.

CHAPTER SEVEN

ASKING FOR
A VERDICT

AFTER YOU'VE HEARD THE ACCUSATION and responded, it's time to receive your verdict. Sometimes the Judge will render a verdict immediately. I've heard many people testify that as soon as they confessed their sin and repented, the Judge banged His gavel and declared them not guilty. In some cases you may need to ask for a specific verdict or decree. Again, the nature of your case and to some degree, your familiarity with the Courts, will determine your actions. There is nothing wrong with simply accepting a not guilty verdict from the Judge. This will be sufficient to remove sickness or other demonic activities. However, it's been my experience that asking for a specific decree can be helpful.

If you're being harassed by a particular spirit, such as a familiar spirit, you may want to ask the judge for a *decree of divorce.* This decree makes it illegal for that spirit to come near or harass you. If your case involves a legal proceeding here on earth, you may ask the judge for a decree that specifies the outcome of that case. If your case involves contractual issues you can ask for a scroll that outlines the terms of the contract.

Along with asking the Judge for a specific decree, you may want to ask for supporting documents that are pertinent to your case. My purpose in asking for documents is twofold: First the documents remind *me* that I've already obtained the victory. I can also use them to remind my adversary that he's been defeated and he had better leave me alone. Both the Old Testament prophets and New Testament Apostles were given documents (scrolls) to eat. There is more than just a symbolic gesture in this. A scroll from heaven is a spiritual law or decree. The intent is that it becomes part of our spirit. To that effect, after I receive a scroll or document I often make a prophetic act and put it inside my spirit.

CHAPTER EIGHT

ENFORCING
THE VERDICT

THE NEXT STEP IS ENFORCING the verdict we've received. In the same way that it's our responsibility to appear in Court and respond to an accusation, it's our responsibility to make certain that the verdict we've received is enforced. This may be the most difficult part of the process and it's the step where most people are likely to fail.

Many times as a result of the verdict, the action that was being taken against us by our adversary will quickly resolve. The sickness will disappear, we'll receive a contract we've been waiting for, or we'll receive notice of a change in legal action. Often times, people are immediately set free of demons. My friends and I see these types of results regularly. But if we're dealing with personal weakness or patterns of behavior that are being exploited by spirits such as lust, there is no guarantee that our adversary will comply with the ruling.

An evil spirit against which you have a decree may refuse to believe that your behavior has changed and it may come back to tempt you a few times. The spirit does so at its own risk. The wager is that you will not take it back to Court to face charges of contempt, but instead, that you'll give in and fall back into the old pattern of behavior.

Evil spirits are master manipulators. They entice us through our thoughts to commit sin. When we take the bait and commit the sin, they accuse us in Court before the Judge. As long as the accusation goes unchallenged, the accuser has grounds to afflict us and obstruct God's plans. It's a vicious cycle and here's how it ends:

Whenever a thought comes to mind that involves an accusation that was brought against you in Court, don't entertain the thought. Take it captive and give it to Jesus. (Any ungodly thought—whether it was mentioned in Court or not—should be handled this way.) The battlefield upon which we wage warfare with the adversary is our mind. Our actions are merely the practical outworking of our thoughts. When we learn to control our thoughts, our behavior follows.

If certain thoughts and behaviors persist after winning a verdict, it's possible that the same spirit is still tempting you. If a spirit you have a decree against continues to harass you, it is now in contempt of Court. In these cases you can ask for the Court to be convened and demand that the spirit appear there to face contempt of Court charges. (Contempt is defined as refusing to obey the orders of a Court.) Inform the Judge that the evil spirit has refused to obey the Court's verdict and ask Him to render judgment against the offending spirit.

As before, you must now enforce the verdict. Take any ungodly thoughts captive and resist them. If the same spirit continues to harass you, take it back to Court to face contempt charges again. The spirit will eventually get tired of the judgments and find someone else to harass. Resist the devil and he will flee.

If you're being harassed by a different spirit, you should convene the Mobile Court and ask for the accusation against you to be heard. As with any other spirit that accuses you, once the accusation has been heard, tell the Judge the blood of Jesus is your defense, remind him that the blood washes away all your sin and ask for a verdict to be rendered against the spirit. Once the verdict has been announced, you may ask for supporting documents. After you receive the documents, you'll need to enforce the verdict.

You can go to the Court of Accusation as often as necessary. Once you've been there a few times, the process becomes easier. All believers should to learn how to go to the Court and represent themselves. It isn't difficult to do and it's part of the process we must go through if we're going to grow into mature children of God.

COURT OF ACCUSATION PROTOCOL

- Ask the Judge to convene the Court.
- Ask for your accuser to appear.
- Ask for the accusation to be heard.
- Agree with the accusation.
- State that the blood of Jesus is your defense.
- Ask for a verdict from the Judge and receive any documents you need.
- Enforce the verdict.

TESTIMONIES FROM THE COURT OF HEAVEN

I'D LIKE TO SHARE THREE testimonies from people who had never been to the Courts of Heaven before. The first testimony is mine. It recounts my first appearance in the Court of Accusation and explains how I came to understand the way the Court works. The two testimonies that immediately follow are ones that friends shared with me.

One day, I became sick with one of the worst viral infections I've ever had. My wife and I prayed to the best of our ability using the strategies we normally use, but the virus would not leave. We had our friends pray for my healing. Despite all of this, the fever, chills, and weakness kept me in bed for four straight days.

On the fourth night of my illness, I was getting ready to go to sleep and my eyes were closed. In my mind's eye, I saw what looked like a bookcase with law books on it. This was a simple image that appeared in my mind. As I looked at the image of the bookcase, I noticed there were a few golden light fixtures nearby. They were not immediately apparent, but the more I focused on the image, the more I began seeing subtle details appear. The scene was reminiscent of my grandfather's house. My grandfather was an attorney. Every bedroom in his house had bookcases lining the walls which held the law books he owned. Looking at the bookcase, I asked my wife, "Why am I seeing something that looks like a courtroom?"

Now, I wasn't certain that what I saw was a Courtroom, much less the Mobile Court of Heaven. I'm often asked if there is a way to know for certain whether something we see in our mind is "real" or if it's "just our imagination." There is no way to know with absolute certainty what you are seeing in the spiritual world is "real." If there were, it would not require faith. I could have written it off as my imagination, but I chose instead to believe that God was inviting me into the Court of Heaven to plead my case concerning my illness.

Though in the vision I saw no one else, once I made the decision to believe I was in Court, my next step was to believe a judge must be present and presiding over my case. I remembered Ian Clayton saying that when you're in the Court of Heaven it's a good idea to ask that your accuser appear, so I asked the Court to summon my accuser. What I saw next was something like a swirling cloud of darkness that was far away at first, but which moved toward me. After about ten seconds it appeared to be beside me in the Courtroom.

I asked that the accusations against me be read. I heard nothing. But as I turned (in my mind) to look at the cloud of darkness, words like "blasphemy" and "liar" appeared to be visible in the cloud. I assumed that these were the charges against me.

I knew I should not dispute the accusations. I said to the Court, "I stand under the blood of Jesus, which cleanses me of all unrighteousness and makes me spotless and blameless in the sight of God." I then I asked for the books to be opened.

At this point, the vision I was seeing in my mind changed. I saw what looked like a stone cliff. I could see there was a small room hidden behind a secret door at the base of the cliff. I saw the door to the hidden room open and a warm glow of light coming from inside the room. Then the door shut.

Next, I saw what looked like a book in front of me. It took a few seconds for the image to become clear. On the edges of the left-hand page I saw a faintly visible flower pattern. There was no decoration on the right-hand page. As I looked at the pages of the book, I could see there was nothing written on them. They were blank.

I assumed that the book was a record of my sins. Because there was nothing written in the book, I took this as an indication that my sins had been removed from the written record in heaven. So I made a short speech to the Court noting that the book showed no record of my sins, because the blood of the lamb had washed them away once and for all. I said that since my sins had been washed away, there was no basis for the affliction the enemy had brought upon me. I asked for a ruling from the Court to have the sickness removed. This was where the visions of the Court ended.

The fever and chills persisted through the night. In the morning the fever left only to return later in the day. By 6:00 pm the following night my temperature was back to normal and I felt much better. I slept well that night, believing the decision from the Court had taken effect. The fever never returned.

I did not see angels, a judge, or any other spiritual beings except for the cloud of darkness that was my accuser. It's not uncommon for people to see angels, a Judge, and Jesus while in Court, but my ability to see them was restricted. I'm not sure why I was unable to see anyone, but I suspect if there were a divine reason, it might be so that I would be forced to believe in something that was not visible. Faith is required when we engage that which is unseen.

Through the entire experience, I heard nothing audible. All communication was done through visions God showed me in my mind and things I either said aloud or thought in my mind.

What follows is a testimony that was sent to me privately by someone who appeared in the Mobile Court after reading my testimony.

I read in one of your articles that a demon can mimic symptoms. I also read the part where you explain the dream about leaving an account with sickness open or closed. And then I received peace.

I read the part on the Courtrooms of Heaven. I went to sleep then and as soon as I closed my eyes, at a distance I saw the Courtroom. I said, "I can't go in, since I'm not invited." Then a tall man in white waved his arm at me and called me to the Courtroom.

I found myself standing before a judge and on my left was a black dark-winged being prosecuting me. The judge looked at me and asked me to state my case. I said "I am guilty, but I ask my advocate the tall man in white (Jesus) my advocate to the Father to take my case for me."

My thoughts then quickly reversed back to a time eight years ago where I promised God I would work for Him in strength like Paul did.

I was back in Court and the Judge hit the wooden hammer and the word "forgiven" appeared before me. The judge then pointed at me very seriously and for a moment I got scared.

He then stood up and came to where Jesus and I were standing, talking to Jesus and pulling out large white strands of pasta like objects. He took it and cut it off by my feet and threw it to the prosecutor.

It ended with me standing outside the Courtroom with a big cherub with a sword of gold.

This final testimony was sent to me by my friend Amanda Leonard:

Two years ago, my son was in a very desperate and tender place. He's only ten now and for years the world had tried to label him—to tell him who he was based on things he liked to do. He's a creative soul. He loves to dance, draw and sing. He's dramatic and expressive.

As a young boy, he liked lots of things that were considered "girl things." He was with me a lot because his daddy worked in law enforcement. At the age of two, he always wanted to dress like a girl. I tried to ignore it, but honestly, I began to get concerned. I would try to shun him away from things that were stereotypically for girls. At the time, I was still dealing with my own identity issues and didn't know how to respond with the Father's heart.

I remember at the age of about six, he came home asking me what the word "gay" meant. I proceeded to tell him that God says the word, "gay" means happy. He said, "Momma, I don't think that's what those boys meant when they called me that." Classmates constantly called him a "girl," even adults would unknowingly say things that referred to him as being "girly" in his nature and mannerisms. Little pictures have big ears and hearts that can break.

Through these years, the Lord had been establishing my identity—who I was in Him. I'm so thankful for that, because, I was able to speak truth into my son, to drown out the lies that had begun to take root. I won't forget the night that my son laid in bed crying out to God, asking God why he felt like he was a girl—almost shouting with sobbing tears. Seeing him this way, ripped my heart out. He told me he knew that he was a boy but he felt like he was a girl, because he liked "girl" things. I told him that God made him a boy and that it was okay that he liked girl things. That didn't make him a girl. I told him that he was very much a boy, created by God. I cried with him that night. I held him and loved him.

I was desperate.

A week before this had happened, I saw a vision of a Mama bird eating and regurgitating up her food and feeding her baby bird in the nest. I didn't know at the time what it meant, so I just held it in my heart. I trusted that the Lord would show me the meaning.

That night, as my son cried out that he felt like a girl, I laid flat on my face, sobbing before the Lord. I was immediately in the spirit and was taken to the courts of heaven. I began to repent for all the fear that I had of my son not being all that the Lord had designed him to be, all the lies that I had believed about him possibly being gay. I was guilty. Everything that Holy Spirit brought to my mind to repent of, I did.

Then the Lord held up a scroll that had my son's name on it and I saw all that he was created to be. I saw words like, "worshipping warrior, artist, creator, inventor, father, musician, sensitive heart," and most importantly "My son." The list went on and on.

The Lord said, "I want you to eat this scroll and regurgitate it back up and feed it to your son. I want him to know all I created him to be. This case of mistaken identity is over!" I saw the vision of the Mama bird *feeding her baby bird. This was me. This was him. This was us.*

From that moment on, everything changed. This was a holy, beautiful masculinity being fully restored for my son, which happened to take place in the courtroom of Heaven. I saw my son through the eyes of the Father. I saw all that the Lord said He would be and was fully convinced. Nothing could any longer shift my view of my son and what the Lord had planned for him. No longer did I define him by what he liked to play with. I saw him and began to speak into him what the Lord showed me that day. The truth of the words that have since been spoken, have been deposited deep within him. He is learning he is a son. He is learning to not be ashamed. He is fully male. He knows how many kids he wants one day and the type of woman he will marry. Even his mannerisms have changed.

CLOSING THOUGHTS

GOING TO THE COURT OF Accusation is an effective strategy to gain victory over our adversary. When a way is found to take back territory the enemy has occupied, there are those who will want to take advantage of it, but feel it isn't their calling, their gifting, or their responsibility. They'll want to have their case heard, but they'll prefer to have someone do it for them.

There are many reasons why we may want to have someone represent us in the Courts of Heaven. We might feel like we'd have no idea what to say. We may not think we'd be able to hear or see what's happening. We may believe these things should be left to professionals—people who know what they're doing. While I believe it's possible to successfully represent someone else in Court, and I've done it on a number of occasions, I think it's best to learn how to represent ourselves.

When you're in Court, you will in nearly every case face your accuser and be confronted with things you've either said or done. While there is no condemnation toward you when the blood of Jesus is your defense, you may need to renounce and/or repent of these things. You may need to do this for yourself and for anyone in your generational line who was involved in this activity. Now ask yourself if this is something you want a stranger doing, or if it would be more appropriate (and more effective) if you were the one doing it.

After a verdict has been rendered and judgment has been passed on your accuser, you should ask for documents from the Court. These documents often become a part of you. They need to be secured by you in your spirit. Is it appropriate to ask someone else to do this for you?

When in Court, you stand before God, who is the Judge of all. Your attorney is Jesus, who paid the ultimate price for your redemption. Here's an opportunity to personally witness the mercy and justice of God. Is it wise for you to turn this over to someone else?

If someone else goes to Court for you today, what happens when the accuser brings a charge against you tomorrow? Or next week? Is it right to expect someone else to represent you in Court for the rest of your life?

The question of who should represent us in the Court of Accusation isn't just about Court cases. It's only the beginning. Spiritual maturity demands that we learn how to operate in even higher Courts, such as the Court of Scribes, the Court of Angels, the Court of Chancellors, and the Divine Council. God desires that we grow up into mature believers. This requires us to administrate His kingdom from our seats of authority in the heavens. No one can do this for us. We must do it ourselves. The only way to learn how to do these things is through personal experience. We must begin representing ourselves in the Court of Accusation because it will lead us on to even more important responsibilities.

I hope this book has helped you understand how to represent yourself in the Court of Accusation. I'm confident that when you appear there, you'll have victory over your adversary.

THANK YOU FOR
PURCHASING THIS BOOK

For inspiring articles and an up-to-date list of my
books, go to my website, **PrayingMedic.com**.
There you will also find links to my Podcasts
and other resources.

Divine Healing Made Simple

Get honest answers to the difficult questions you have about healing and the supernatural:

- Why are my prayers ineffective when I ask God to heal someone?
- Many people have prayed for my healing— so why am I still not healed?
- Does God want me to learn a lesson through physical suffering and sickness?
- I was miraculously healed through prayer— why have my symptoms returned?

Get the answers to these questions... and many more.

In his down-to-earth style, Praying Medic presents a solid case that all believers have power and authority from God for healing. Miracles are happening every day through the prayers of average men and women on the street and in workplaces. With a little instruction, you too can learn how to release God's healing power. Exercises at the end of key chapters will help you develop your ability. With insight on many other topics including making disciples, deliverance, words of knowledge, and how God speaks to you through your dreams, this book celebrates what God is doing and shows you how miracles can become part of your everyday life.

This book is part of a series called **The Kingdom of God Made Simple** — a self-study course designed to train believers to live the life offered to them as heirs of God's kingdom.

Seeing in the Spirit Made Simple

Is "seeing in the spirit" only for a few people—or can anyone do it?

If you want to see angels, demons and the heavenly realms, but have been told you don't have the gift of seeing in the spirit, this book is for you. For years we've been told that seeing in the spirit is a gift given to only a few special people or an anointing that must be imparted to us by a man or woman of God. In this book, Praying Medic presents biblical and physiological evidence to prove that seeing in the spirit is not reserved for only a few special people, but is possible for everyone.

With the same down-to-earth teaching style he used in **Divine Healing Made Simple** and **Hearing God's Voice Made Simple**, the author provides Bible-based teaching, dozens of testimonies, and illustrations that reveal the truth about seeing in the spirit. He includes exercises at the end of key chapters to help you improve your spiritual vision. Whether you're a seasoned seer or a newbie, you'll learn from the experiences and insights shared by the author. Not only will you develop better spiritual eyesight, but your relationship with God will grow too.

This book is part of a series called **The Kingdom of God Made Simple** —
a self-study course designed to train believers to live the
life offered to them as heirs of God's kingdom.

Hearing God's Voice Made Simple

Is God Really Speaking?
Yes—and you can learn to hear Him.

Today, many are skeptical that God is speaking or that we can know with certainty we're hearing Him accurately. **Hearing God's Voice Made Simple** makes the case that God is speaking and that we can learn to hear Him. As you read this book, you may even discover that God has been speaking to you all along but you simply didn't know how to hear Him.

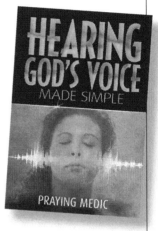

With the same straightforward, down-to-earth style used in the best-sellers **Divine Healing Made Simple** and **Seeing in the Spirit Made Simple**, Praying Medic teaches about the many ways in which God speaks. You'll find practical exercises at the end of key chapters to help develop your ability to sense what God is saying to you. Whether you're skilled at hearing God's voice, or more of a novice, this book will show you ways of hearing from God that you may not have considered—and you'll also learn what to do with the things God says.

This book is part of a series called **The Kingdom of God Made Simple** —
a self-study course designed to train believers to live the
life offered to them as heirs of God's kingdom.

Traveling in the Spirit Made Simple

Is spiritual travel "astral projection" or is it a biblical practice used for God's purposes?

If you've been taught that traveling in the spirit is unbiblical or is only used by the New Age or the occult, this book is for you. The author examines accounts from the Bible which demonstrate that the prophets and apostles traveled in the spirit. He compares astral projection with Christian spiritual travel and proves that they are not the same thing. Far from being an occult practice, spiritual travel is actually a tool given to us by God to accomplish His divine purposes.

With the same down-to-earth teaching style used in **Seeing in the Spirit Made Simple** and **Divine Healing Made Simple**, Praying Medic provides Bible-based teaching, dozens of testimonies and illustrations that will help even the least experienced believer understand spiritual travel. Exercises are provided at the end of key chapters. Traveling in the spirit can help you in healing, deliverance and intercession, but most importantly, it will help you know God in a more personal way.

This book is part of a series called **The Kingdom of God Made Simple** — a self-study course designed to train believers to live the life offered to them as heirs of God's kingdom.

Emotional Healing in 3 Easy Steps

If you've been through counseling, prayer, or deliverance, but you're still plagued with painful emotions like shame, guilt, fear or anger, this book can help you get free of those emotions once and for all.

This isn't another nice-sounding, but powerless self-help book. It's not filled with pop-psychology. It's a field-tested method of erasing traumatic wounds in your soul and releasing the painful emotions associated with them. And it doesn't require long hours of prayer or counseling. You can do it yourself and it will only take a few minutes.

If you're ready to ditch your emotional baggage, put your past behind you, and get off the emotional roller-coaster you've been riding, you're just 30 minutes away from a new you.

Are you ready?

My Craziest Adventures with God - Volume 1
The Spiritual Journal of a Former Atheist Paramedic

Does God speak today? Would He heal the sick or work miracles through you—even if you feel "average" or not particularly gifted?

Not long ago, Praying Medic was an average guy who sat in a church pew every Sunday wondering if there was more to the Christian life than this. After losing his job, being divorced and being kicked out of his church, it seemed like his entire world was going up in flames. Then one night in a dream, God asked him to pray for his patients. When he awoke in the morning he knew nothing would ever be the same.

Come along on these intriguing adventures as an ordinary paramedic confronts his own skepticism and fear and learns how to hear the voice of God. Get to know Praying Medic, the author, through these stories from his personal spiritual diary. Watch as he learns how to pray for his patients and for strangers in the marketplace.

God's goodness and sense of humor are revealed in these true stories. And you'll witness the transformational power of God as it changes a hardened skeptic into a man of real faith. These stories won't just encourage you—they'll teach you how to live daily in the fullness of God's kingdom.

My Craziest Adventures with God - Volume 2
The Spiritual Journal of a Former Atheist Paramedic

Picking up where Volume One left off, Praying Medic and his wife are back with more stories about their supernatural adventures with God.

Not long ago they were a couple of atheists. Then they met God. After learning about the authority and power believers have been given to heal the sick and work miracles, they began praying with people wherever they went and their lives have never been the same.

Come along on their adventures with Jesus and the Holy Spirit. Discover how an unexpected invitation to travel to Brisbane, Australia, brought them into working on the streets— alongside dedicated local church volunteers— praying for men and women in homeless shelters and on the streets.

Watch as these ordinary believers see the sick healed, the mentally ill set free, and demonic forces beaten. From healing, to automotive miracles, time alteration, and financial miracles, nothing is off limits for God.

You'll be laughing one minute and crying the next as the extravagant love of God is poured into the lives of the people you'll meet in these stories.

A Kingdom View of Economic Collapse

If you'd like to learn about economic collapse, but you're tired of being lured into investing scams, and hearing warnings about God's judgment, this may be the book you've been looking for.

In his usual no-nonsense style, Praying Medic gives readers a crash course in economics and finance, explaining things in terms the average person can understand. He provides an overview of historic cases of economic collapse and determines which nations are at risk today. He examines the cause of the recent Greek debt crisis and shares the lessons to be learned from it. He shares a number of prophetic dreams about economics and finance, and offers suggestions about how we might rebuild after a collapse, if one were to happen. The final chapter discusses how the kingdom of God ought to respond to crisis.

Topics covered in this book:
- God's purposes for economic crisis.
- Why governments print so much money.
- A prophetic look at our economic future.
- A simple lesson on finance and economics.
- The role of the International Monetary Fund.
- A look at historic cases of economic collapse.
- How central banks and the Federal Reserve operate.
- Which nations are currently at risk for economic collapse.
- How we might rebuild in the aftermath of an economic collapse.
- How the Greek debt crisis happened and lessons to be learned from it.

American Sniper: Lessons in Spiritual Warfare

Drawing upon scenes from the popular film American Sniper, Praying Medic gives readers a look inside the mind of a well-prepared kingdom soldier.

Relying on the use of analogy and symbolism, the author compares the life of a Navy SEAL to the life of a believer. The book closely follows the script of the film. With each scene the author illustrates principles of spiritual warfare, drawing from his own life experiences and from many spiritual dreams he's had.

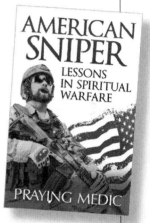

The goal of this book is to help believers assess their state spiritual preparedness and identify any deficiencies they might have. Resources are recommended for further training and equipping, if needed.

Because so many lives have been devastated by the kind of emotional trauma portrayed in the film, the last chapter includes a simple approach to healing emotional trauma that can be used by virtually anyone.

Whether you're in a position of church leadership or just someone who wishes to be better trained and equipped for ministry, this book will add a few more tools to your arsenal.